Autumn Nights, Winter Mornings

A COLLECTION OF COLD-WEATHER COMFORT FOODS

BY BARBARA SCOTT-GOODMAN

WITH MARY GOODBODY

ILLUSTRATIONS BY ANDREA BROOKS

CHRONICLE BOOKS

SAN FRANCISCO

For Lester,
Zan, and Isabelle

Many thanks again to Bill LeBlond, Leslie Jonath, Laura Lovett,
and all the terrific people at Chronicle Books; to my agent Bob Cornfield,
to Deborah Callan for recipe testing, and to my friend and collaborator,
Mary Goodbody, who is always so wonderful to work with.

Library of Congress Cataloging in Publication Data:

Scott-Goodman, Barbara.
Autumn nights, winter mornings: a collection of cold-weather
comfort foods / by Barbara Scott-Goodman with Mary Goodbody ;
illustrations by Andrea Brooks.
p. cm.
includes index.
ISBN 0-8118-1038-0
1. Cookery. 2. Autumn 3. Winter 4. Entertaining.
I. Goodbody, Mary. II. Title.
TX714. S388 1995
641.5—dc20 95-1569
CIP

Printed in Hong Kong.

Distributed in Canada by Raincoast Books, 8680 Cambie St., Vancouver, B.C. V6P 6M9
10 9 8 7 6 5 4 3 2 1

Chronicle Books
275 Fifth Street
San Francisco, CA 94103

CONTENTS

*W*hen autumn arrives and I find myself back in New York City after a long, lingering summer on the easternmost tip of Long Island, I can't help but feel energized and eager to tackle the busy months ahead. I yearn to catch up with friends I have missed during the summer, to poke around my favorite shops and local markets, and to restock my kitchen—where I spend so much of my time—with fresh herbs and spices, bottles of fruity green olive oil and rich balsamic vinegar, jars of mustard, honey, and syrup, and sacks of rice and beans—the staples that to me define home cooking. This is when I happily plan small informal dinner parties with no-fuss menus based on simple, full-flavored foods.

I regularly visit my local farmer's market and travel uptown to the Union Square Farmers' Market a couple times a week just to see what glories the farmers are offering. In September I can still get sweet, tender corn and ripe, juicy tomatoes, and summer squash, zucchini, and newly dug potatoes are at their peak. I use these to make Indian Summer Vegetable Soup, letting its sunny flavors ease me out of summer and into fall. Later in this golden season, I look for fresh beet greens attached to tender beets, earthy mushrooms, crunchy apples, crisp turnips and parsnips, fennel, bell peppers, broccoli rabe, succulent red plums, and fall's finest pears. Who can help being influenced by the bounty of fall's harvest? As in the summer and spring, I cook according to what looks best and freshest.

Once my menu is set, I invite good friends to join my family for casual meals. These are the friends who enjoy spending time with me in the kitchen as I complete last-minute preparations, who don't mind chopping some extra parsley or opening the wine so it can breathe on the countertop. We draw the blinds against the darkening, nippy evening and eat by candlelight. Outside the city bustles with the frenzy that is New York; inside we enjoy good, warm food, full-bodied wine, and plenty of laughter.

*a*utumn slips into the holidays, which so easily are consumed by family, annual rituals, and giddy anticipation. Knowing that I have connected with friends earlier in the season helps center me as I prepare holiday meals with familiar contentment. The recipes included in this book are not traditional holiday fare, although some would be lovely served on Thanksgiving Day or Christmas morning—and New Year's Day is a perfect day for brunch. But it's when the holidays are behind us that I most often invite people in for brunch.

Winter brings its own rhythm of cold, bright mornings when the sun dances off the snow (even in New York!), gradually lengthening days, and weekends that stretch longer than at other times of year. Relaxed, country-style breakfasts and festive brunch parties are wonderful for family entertaining, and I love to orchestrate such get-togethers—as long as they don't begin too early! On these weekend mornings, I rise first, brew a pot of strong coffee, and bake biscuits or scones, letting their homey aromas fill the house. Just as these scents rouse my family from their sleepy nests, so do they welcome friends and neighbors for a leisurely gathering. Brunch is a meal for hearty foods, such as hash, slow-cooked potatoes, and frittatas. It's great, too, for pancakes and French toast, especially if children are in the crowd. And it's a splendid excuse to make a delectable tart of smoked salmon or potato gratin with scrambled eggs. On these frosty mornings, my daughters love creamy hot chocolate or more exotic hot white chocolate as much as their parents appreciate spicy Bloody Marys and refreshing citrus mimosas. Brunch provides the opportunity to indulge. And, as always, food carefully prepared is the best way to bring together those who mean the most to us.

a u t u m n

n i g h t s

Indian Summer Vegetable Soup

Serves 6

This delicious soup combines the best of fall's early harvests, when tomatoes, zucchini, and corn are still available and new potatoes and squash are at their best. At the Union Square Farmers' Market in New York, I can get good tomatoes and corn right into early October—and so I can make this aromatic soup with some regularity. I love it with Red Pepper Corn Bread (see page 14) or a loaf of crusty peasant bread from the Farmers' Market or a local bakery.

2 tablespoons olive oil
2 cloves garlic, thinly sliced
1 medium onion, thinly sliced
2 medium carrots, peeled and diced
2 medium ribs celery, diced
6 cups chicken stock, preferably homemade
4 cups water
2 large garden tomatoes or 5 or 6 plum tomatoes, peeled, seeded, and
coarsely chopped, or 5 or 6 canned plum tomatoes, drained and chopped
4 unpeeled small new potatoes, cut into ½-inch dice (about 1½ cups)
1 small zucchini, peeled and cut into ¼-inch dice
1 small yellow squash, peeled and cut into ¼-inch dice
2 cups fresh corn kernels (from 2 or 3 large ears sweet corn)
or frozen corn kernels
4 ounces green beans, ends trimmed and cut into 1-inch pieces
¾ cup penne pasta
½ cup chopped fresh parsley
¼ cup coarsely chopped fresh basil
Freshly ground black pepper to taste
Freshly grated Parmesan cheese for serving

1. Heat the olive oil in a large stockpot over medium–high heat. Add the garlic and onion, cover, and cook for about 5 minutes until the onions soften. Add the carrots and celery, cover, and cook for about 10 minutes longer until the vegetables are tender.

2. Add the chicken stock and water, bring to a boil, and reduce the heat to medium. Add the tomatoes, potatoes, zucchini, and yellow squash and simmer for about 15 minutes, stirring occasionally.

3. Stir in the corn and green beans, reduce the heat to low, and cook for about 10 minutes. *The soup may be cooked up to this point and refrigerated until just before serving.*

4. Add the pasta and simmer for about 8 minutes until cooked but still firm. *If the soup has been refrigerated, bring it to a simmer before cooking the pasta.*

5. Stir in the parsley and basil and season with pepper. Ladle into shallow soup bowls and pass the grated cheese at the table.

Black Bean Soup with Madeira and Lemon

Serves 6

I love to make soup, especially this thick, wonderfully rich, full-flavored black bean soup. Serve it with a green salad, a crusty baguette, and a little wine. Who could ask for more?

3 tablespoons olive oil
1 onion, chopped
3 ribs celery with leaves, chopped
1½ cups dried black beans, picked over and rinsed
6 cups chicken stock, preferably homemade
Salt and freshly ground black pepper to taste
1 tablespoon celery seed
2 tablespoons fresh lemon juice, or to taste
2 to 4 tablespoons dry sherry, or to taste
Lemon slices for garnish
Chopped fresh parsley for garnish

1. Heat the oil in a large, heavy saucepan over medium heat and sauté the onion and celery for 8 to 10 minutes until tender. Add the beans and stock. Bring to a boil over high heat, reduce the heat to medium-low, cover, and simmer for 2½ to 3 hours until the beans are tender. Remove from the heat and set aside to cool for about 30 minutes.

2. Purée the cooled beans in a food processor or blender. You may have to do this in 2 or 3 batches.

3. Return the puréed soup to the pan and reheat, seasoning with salt, pepper, and celery seed. Stir until the soup thickens slightly and is heated through. If it is too thick, add a little stock. Stir in the lemon juice and sherry. Serve in bowls, garnished with lemon slices and parsley.

Note: Because the beans cook for 2½ to 3 hours, they do not need to be soaked or precooked.

Wild Mushroom Soup

Serves 6 as a main course, 8 as a first course

Dried wild mushrooms give this soup a wonderfully rich, woodsy flavor. The mushrooms may be hard to find (as well as being expensive), but a few go a long way and their soaking liquid provides incomparable flavor. Although white button mushrooms may be used for the fresh mushrooms, I like to use intensely flavorful cremini mushrooms.

2 ounces dried porcini mushrooms
1½ cups lukewarm water
2 tablespoons unsalted butter
1 tablespoon olive oil
3 large leeks (white and green parts), rinsed and diced (about 3 cups)
2 medium onions, thinly sliced
1 pound fresh mushrooms, preferably cremini, stemmed and thinly sliced
3 tablespoons flour
4 cups chicken stock, preferably homemade
2 cups water
Salt and freshly ground black pepper to taste
½ cup Madeira wine
½ cup plus 3 tablespoons chopped fresh parsley
Sour cream for garnish

1. Put the dried mushrooms in a bowl and add the lukewarm water. Soak for about 30 minutes. Lift out the mushrooms and set aside but do not discard the water. Strain the soaking water through a sieve lined with paper towels or a coffee filter and set aside.

2. In a stockpot, heat the butter and oil and over medium heat until the butter melts. Add the leeks and onions and cook for about 10 minutes, stirring often, until tender.

3. Set aside about ½ cup of the sliced fresh mushrooms to use for garnish. Add the remaining fresh mushrooms to the pot and cook for about 5 minutes until softened. Sprinkle with the flour and cook for an additional 5 minutes, stirring occasionally.

4. Add the chicken stock, water, soaked dried mushrooms, and the reserved strained soaking water. Add the salt and several generous grindings of pepper. Bring to a boil, reduce the heat, and simmer, uncovered, for about 5 minutes, stirring occasionally, until the soup is heated through. Remove the soup from the heat and let it cool for about 10 minutes.

5. Purée the soup in batches in a food processor or blender until nearly smooth; the soup will retain some texture from the mushrooms. Return the soup to the pot and heat over low heat for about 5 minutes.

6. Stir in the wine and ½ cup of the parsley and cook, stirring occasionally, for about 5 minutes.

7. Ladle the soup into shallow bowls and top each serving with a dollop of sour cream, a few slices of mushrooms, and some chopped parsley.

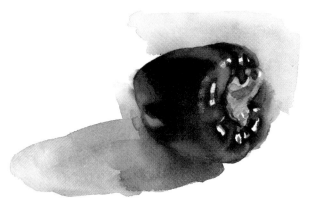

Red Pepper Corn Bread

Serves 6 to 8

The roasted red peppers provide lovely, rich flavor, making this homey bread delicious with hot soup or as an accompaniment to pot roast or braised pork. If you prefer plain corn bread, omit the red peppers. Either way, it's a winner.

2 medium red bell peppers
2 tablespoons unsalted butter
1 cup stone-ground yellow cornmeal
1 cup unbleached all-purpose flour
2 tablespoons sugar
2 teaspoons baking powder
½ teaspoon salt
2 large eggs
1 cup milk

1. Preheat the broiler.

2. Put the peppers on a rack a few inches from the heat source and roast until charred black, turning several times during roasting. Remove from the broiler and put in a small paper bag. Fold the bag closed and let the peppers cool inside the bag for at least 20 minutes.

3. When the peppers are cool, rub the charred black skin from the flesh. Cut the peppers in half, scrape off the seeds, and cut off the stems. Cut the flesh into ½-inch pieces and set aside. You will have about 1 cup.

4. Preheat the oven to 400°F.

5. Put the butter in an 8-inch-square pan and melt in the oven while preparing the corn bread batter. Watch it carefully to prevent burning.

6. In a large bowl, whisk together the cornmeal, flour, sugar, baking powder, and salt.

7. Mix the eggs with the milk. Pour the egg-milk mixture into the cornmeal mixture and stir with a fork until well blended. Stir in the red peppers.

8. Take the pan from the oven and scrape the batter into it. Stir gently around the edges of the pan to incorporate the melted butter. Smooth the top of the batter. Bake for 20 to 23 minutes until the bread pulls away from the sides of the pan, the top is set, and a toothpick inserted in the center comes out clean. Let cool on a wire rack. Cut into squares and serve.

Blue Cheese Caesar Salad
(Not-So-Classic Caesar Salad)

Serves 6 as an appetizer, 4 as a main course

Classic Caesar salad is composed of romaine lettuce, Parmesan cheese, and a dressing made from oil, fresh lemon juice, Worcestershire sauce, and a raw egg. Most people also think the salad includes anchovies. I recently read that the salty fishes were not included in the original recipe—invented in the 1920s by restaurateur Caesar Cardini—but were added to a recipe printed on the label of a bottle of Worcestershire sauce. So much for the classics! My version includes homemade croutons and omits the raw egg altogether. It's topped with blue cheese and the anchovies are optional. Serve this as a meal in itself with crusty bread and a good bottle of red Italian wine, or as a prelude to a more elaborate dinner.

¾ cup extra-virgin olive oil
4 large cloves garlic, peeled
4 cups ½-inch cubes French or Italian bread (about half a baguette)
Salt to taste
1 large or 2 medium heads romaine lettuce
Juice of 1 lemon
¼ cup Worcestershire sauce
½ cup (2 ounces) freshly grated Parmesan cheese
Freshly ground black pepper to taste
6 ounces blue cheese, crumbled
8 anchovy fillets, drained (optional)

1. The day before making the salad, mix the olive oil and garlic together in a jar, cover, and set aside. For more intense garlic flavor, cut one of the cloves in half.

2. In a large skillet, heat ¼ cup of the garlic-flavored oil over medium heat. Add the bread cubes, sprinkle with a little salt, and sauté for about 15 minutes, shaking and turning to coat the bread until golden. Lift the croutons from the pan with a slotted spoon and set aside to drain on paper towels.

3. Tear the romaine lettuce leaves into good-sized pieces and put them in a large salad bowl. Add 6 tablespoons of the oil and toss to coat the leaves thoroughly. Add the lemon juice and Worcestershire sauce and toss again. Season to taste with salt.

4. Add the Parmesan cheese and the remaining 2 tablespoons oil and toss. Toss in the croutons and season to taste with pepper.

5. Arrange the salad on chilled dinner plates and top with blue cheese and anchovies, if desired. Serve immediately.

Warm Potato and White Bean Salad

Serves 6

Warm salads and chilly nights are made for each other. I like this as a first course or part of an antipasto platter that includes lots of steamed vegetables. I recommend starting with dried beans, since canned beans are too mushy for the salad. For easy assembly, you can prepare the separate components (beans, potatoes, watercress) well ahead of time, and then toss them together at the last minute.

1 cup dried white beans, picked over and rinsed
2 cups chicken stock, preferably homemade
2 cups water
1 whole onion, peeled
2 small carrots, peeled and cut in half crosswise
12 unpeeled small red new potatoes (about 1¼ pounds)
1 small red onion, quartered and thinly sliced
1 bunch watercress, stemmed (about 2 loosely packed cups)
2 tablespoons red wine vinegar
7 tablespoons extra-virgin olive oil
Salt and freshly ground pepper to taste
2 dozen niçoise, kalamata, or Gaeta olives

1. Put the beans in a bowl and add cold water to cover by about 2 inches. Soak for 6 to 8 hours or overnight. Change the water once or twice during soaking.

2. Drain the beans and put them in a stockpot. Add the chicken stock, water, onion, and carrots. Bring to a boil over high heat, reduce the heat, cover, and simmer for 50 to 60 minutes, stirring occasionally, until just tender. Be careful not to overcook or boil the beans.

3. Drain and rinse the beans. Discard the onion and carrots. Place the beans in a large bowl.

4. In a large saucepan, cook the potatoes in boiling salted water to cover for about 20 minutes until tender. Drain and set aside.

5. When the potatoes are cool enough to handle, peel and cut them into ½-inch cubes. Add them to the beans. Stir in the red onion and the watercress and gently toss.

6. Add the vinegar and olive oil and season with salt and pepper. Stir in the olives. Adjust the seasoning and serve immediately.

Note: To avoid long soaking, prepare the beans by the quick-soak method: Put the rinsed beans in a large pot and cover with 3 cups of hot water. Bring to a boil over high heat and boil, uncovered, for 2 minutes. Remove the pot from the heat, cover, and set aside for 1 hour. Drain and rinse the beans and put them in a stockpot. Proceed with the recipe, beginning with the second sentence in step 2.

Braised Roast of Pork with Autumn Root Vegetables

Serves 6

I make this pork dish for special dinner parties. The roast is first browned and then gently braised in its natural juices with vegetables. I cook it with lots of garlic, which makes the kitchen smell wonderful! Sliced and served with the vegetables, it tastes as good as it looks—and, to my mind, says "autumn" loud and clear.

2 tablespoons safflower oil
One 3½- to 4-pound boneless center-cut pork loin
Salt and freshly ground black pepper to taste
3 medium white turnips (about 2 pounds), peeled and quartered
3 medium white onions, quartered
4 medium carrots, peeled and cut into 1-inch rounds
12 cloves garlic, peeled and left whole
½ teaspoon dried thyme
6 fresh parsley sprigs
2 tablespoons water

1. Preheat the oven to 350°F.

2. Heat the oil in a large skillet over medium heat. Add the meat to the pan and brown for about 20 minutes, turning to brown all sides. Season with salt and pepper, remove the meat from the skillet and set it aside.

3. Put the turnips, onions, carrots, and garlic in the skillet and cook for about 10 minutes, stirring occasionally, until lightly browned. You may have to do this in batches. Add the thyme and parsley. If the vegetables

seem dry, add 1 or 2 tablespoons of water to the skillet. Transfer the vegetables to a large roasting pan and then place the meat on top of the vegetables.

4. Add the water and cover with a sheet of aluminum foil. Cover the roaster with its lid. If it does not have a lid, cover with another sheet of foil. Roast for 1 hour and 15 minutes, basting the roast every 20 minutes, until a meat thermometer inserted into the center of the roast registers 160°F.

5. Slice the roast into ½-inch slices. Arrange the vegetables on a warm serving platter and lay the slices on top. Spoon the pan juices over the meat and vegetables and serve immediately.

Chicken Sautéed with Apples, Shallots, and Ginger

Serves 6

This dish embodies the essence of good, simple comfort food. My family loves it during the week, particularly after a weekend trip to an orchard for crisp autumn apples, and I also like to cook it for guests. For a perfect fall supper, serve the chicken with wild rice, a green salad, and Brussels sprouts.

2 tablespoons extra-virgin olive oil
Two 2½- to 3-pound chickens, cut into 8 pieces each,
rinsed and patted dry
12 shallots, thinly sliced
2 cloves garlic, thinly sliced
One 3- to 4-inch piece peeled fresh ginger, thinly sliced
(about 2 tablespoons)
4 firm sweet apples, such as McIntosh or Empire, cored and
cut into ¼-inch slices (about 4 cups)
¼ teaspoon ground cinnamon
¾ cup dry white wine
½ cup apple cider
Salt and freshly ground black pepper to taste

1. Heat the oil in a large skillet over medium-high heat. Add half the chicken pieces and brown for 10 to 12 minutes, turning to brown both sides. Lift the chicken from the pan, put in a large baking dish, and set aside. Cook the remaining chicken and set it aside.

2. Preheat the oven to 350°F.

3. Pour off all but 1 tablespoon of fat from the skillet. Add the shallots, garlic, ginger, apples, and cinnamon and sauté for about 5 minutes over medium–high heat. Add the wine and cider and cook for 3 to 5 minutes, stirring to scrape up any brown bits from the bottom of the pan. Season with salt and pepper and pour over the browned chicken. Cover the baking dish with aluminum foil and bake for 45 to 50 minutes until the chicken is tender.

4. To serve, remove the foil and serve directly from the baking dish, or transfer the chicken and sauce to a warm serving platter.

Risotto with Broccoli Rabe and Parmesan

Serves 6

Risotto, the delectable Italian rice dish, is absolutely wonderful teamed with broccoli rabe. You could also use broccoli, but I recommend the more assertive, pleasantly bitter green—it infuses the risotto with big, bold flavor. Risotto can be tricky to make, because while each grain of rice should be separate, the creamy sauce made from broth, butter, and cheese must bind the rice. To achieve the proper balance, take care not to overcook the rice, and stir the risotto vigilantly during cooking. Try to use Italian arborio rice or another medium-grain rice. True risotto lovers note that the last person served may find his or her risotto less perfect than the first person served. This version is delicious regardless of the dining-table pecking order!

6 to 7 cups chicken stock, preferably homemade
1 tablespoon unsalted butter
2 tablespoons extra-virgin olive oil
½ cup finely chopped shallots
3 cloves garlic, thinly sliced
2 cups arborio rice
1 bunch (1 to 1½ pounds) broccoli rabe, tough stems discarded and chopped into 1-inch pieces
½ cup finely chopped parsley
3 tablespoons freshly grated Parmesan cheese, plus more for serving
2 tablespoons fresh lemon juice
Salt and freshly ground black pepper to taste

1. In a large saucepan, bring the stock to a boil over high heat. Reduce the heat to maintain a simmer.

2. Meanwhile, heat the butter and oil in a Dutch oven set over medium heat. Add the shallots and garlic and sauté for about 5 minutes until soft. Add the rice and stir with a wooden spoon until the rice is well coated with butter and oil.

3. Slowly add the simmering broth to the rice, a ladleful at a time. Stir constantly with the wooden spoon to prevent the rice from sticking. As soon as one ladle of broth is absorbed by the rice, add the next. The entire process will take 15 to 20 minutes, and the rice should be tender but still firm.

4. Add the broccoli rabe, parsley, the 3 tablespoons Parmesan cheese, and the lemon juice. Stir for about 5 minutes, tasting to test for doneness. The broccoli rabe will be crisp-tender. Season to taste with salt and pepper and serve immediately with grated Parmesan cheese.

Shellfish Stew

Serves 6

For everyone who likes seafood, this is a terrific dinner-party dish. You can make the broth well ahead of time and refrigerate or freeze it. Add some crusty bread, a green salad, and chilled white wine, and you have a complete meal.

2 tablespoons olive oil
4 cloves garlic, thinly sliced
2 medium onions, thinly sliced (about 2 cups)
One 28-ounce can plum tomatoes
1 cup dry white wine
1 cup bottled clam juice
1 teaspoon fennel seed
1 teaspoon dried thyme
½ teaspoon saffron threads
2 bay leaves
Freshly ground black pepper to taste
12 small new potatoes (about 3 pounds), quartered (4 to 5 cups)
24 littleneck clams
1 pound mussels
8 ounces medium shrimp, peeled and deveined (at least 18 shrimp)
½ cup chopped fresh parsley, plus more for garnish

1. Heat the olive oil in a large stockpot over medium-low heat. Add the garlic and onions and cook for 10 to 15 minutes until softened.

2. Add the tomatoes and their juice, the wine, clam juice, fennel seed, thyme, saffron, bay leaves, and pepper. Bring to a boil, partially cover, reduce the heat and simmer for 40 minutes, stirring occasionally. Keep

the broth warm, *or cover and refrigerate for up to 2 days, or freeze the broth for up to 1 month.*

3. Put the potatoes in a large saucepan and cover with cold water. Lightly salt the water and bring it to a boil over high heat. Cover, reduce the heat to medium-low, and cook for 15 to 20 minutes until the potatoes are fork tender. Drain and keep warm.

4. Bring the broth back to a boil and add the clams, mussels, shrimp, and parsley. Cover and cook over high heat for 8 to 10 minutes until the clams and mussels open and the shrimp turn pink. Discard the bay leaves and any unopened clams or mussels.

5. Spoon the potatoes into 6 shallow soup bowls. Ladle the seafood stew over the potatoes. Garnish with parsley.

Beets with Balsamic Vinaigrette, Pecans, and Beet Greens

Serves 6

During the cold months, I find warm vegetables flavored with a piquant vinaigrette are a wonderful alternative to salads. Beets take beautifully to this treatment, which is wonderful news, since beets are among my favorite autumn vegetables. When buying them, look for those topped with fresh-looking beet greens. This not only promises fresh beets, but is especially important because the greens are part of this dish.

2 bunches (about 2 pounds) beets (about 8 medium beets),
with their greens
2 tablespoons vegetable or peanut oil
2 tablespoons balsamic vinegar
2 tablespoons fresh lemon juice
6 tablespoons extra-virgin olive oil
Salt and freshly ground black pepper to taste
3 tablespoons coarsely chopped pecans

1. Cut the beet greens from the beets, discarding any wilted or dried greens, and trim the stems. Rinse, dry, and set the greens aside.

2. Peel the beets, quarter them, and cut them into ¼-inch slices. Place in a vegetable steamer over boiling water, cover, and cook over medium-high heat for 15 to 20 minutes until just tender.

3. Heat the vegetable oil in a skillet over medium-high heat. Sauté the beet greens for about 3 minutes until wilted. Put in a serving dish, set aside, and keep warm.

4. Combine the vinegar and lemon juice in a small bowl. Whisk in the olive oil and season with salt and pepper.

5. To serve, spoon the warm steamed beets over the beet greens. Drizzle with the vinaigrette and scatter the nuts over the beets. Serve immediately.

Grilled Fennel, Peppers, and Potatoes

Serves 6

Grilled vegetables are so delicious, it's a shame to relegate them to summertime cooking. Make these all year long, on an outdoor or stovetop grill. You can cook them under the broiler with superb results, too. These vegetables are precooked and then grilled just long enough to give them a good flavor. I like to serve these with barbecued chicken or grilled lamb.

1 fennel bulb, cut into 6 or more ¼-inch slices
Juice of 1 lemon
1 teaspoon red wine vinegar
½ cup plus 2 tablespoons extra-virgin olive oil
2 teaspoons chopped fresh rosemary
Salt and freshly ground black pepper to taste
2 medium Idaho or russet potatoes (about 1 pound)
2 red bell peppers, seeded, deveined, and quartered

1. Preheat the oven to 350°F.

2. Line a large roasting pan with aluminum foil. Lay the fennel slices in a single layer in the roasting pan.

3. In a small bowl, whisk together the lemon juice and vinegar. Slowly add the ½ cup olive oil, whisking constantly. Stir in the rosemary and season with salt and pepper. Pour over the fennel and bake for 10 minutes. Turn the fennel and bake 10 minutes longer. Lift the fennel from the marinade and set aside. Leave the marinade in the roasting pan.

4. Meanwhile, bring a large pot of lightly salted water to a boil. Boil the potatoes for about 20 minutes until just tender. Drain and rinse under cold running water. When the potatoes are cool enough to handle, peel and cut into at least twelve ¼-inch slices. Set aside.

5. Toss the red peppers with the remaining 2 tablespoons olive oil. Set aside.

6. Prepare a charcoal or gas grill or preheat the broiler. Spray a grilling grid or screen with vegetable oil spray and lay the potatoes on it. When the coals are medium hot, grill the potatoes for 8 minutes, turning once or twice. Add the fennel and peppers and continue grilling, turning often, for 10 to 12 minutes until the vegetables are nicely browned and tender. If you must grill in batches, transfer the cooked vegetables to the roasting pan with the marinade and keep warm. If broiling, the cooking times will be the same, but watch the fennel and peppers closely to prevent burning.

7. Serve the vegetables on a warm platter, drizzled with the marinade.

Caramelized Root Vegetables

Serves 6

Slow-cooked autumn vegetables are an ideal side dish for a simple cool-weather meal. The gentle oven roasting allows them to caramelize, which accentuates the vegetables' natural sugars to give them a full, rounded flavor. In this recipe, I toss potatoes, carrots, parsnips, and shallots with fruity olive oil and roast them for up to two hours. Great for dinner-party advance planning— great tasting, too.

2 pounds unpeeled small red new potatoes (8 to 10 potatoes),
halved or quartered
12 shallots (about 6 ounces)
6 carrots, peeled and cut into 1-inch lengths
4 parsnips (about 1 pound), peeled and cut into 1-inch rounds
3 tablespoons extra-virgin olive oil, plus more for drizzling (optional)
1 tablespoon fresh rosemary leaves, or 1 teaspoon dried rosemary
1 tablespoon coarse salt
Freshly ground black pepper to taste

1. Preheat the oven to 300°F.

2. In a roasting pan, toss the potatoes, shallots, carrots, and parsnips with the olive oil, rosemary, salt, and pepper.

3. Roast for 1¾ to 2 hours, until the vegetables are fork tender, tossing them 2 or 3 times during roasting to keep them from sticking and to blend the flavors.

4. Heap the roasted vegetables in a shallow bowl or on a large platter. Drizzle with a bit of extra olive oil, if desired. Serve warm or at room temperature.

Bread Pudding with Red Plums

Serves 6

Bread pudding is a simple and satisfying dessert to make on a chilly autumn night. I've tried this with various types of plums and found that red plums—readily available during the fall—are the best. This is especially good served warm with a scoop of vanilla ice cream or whipped cream. My daughter Zan, who is a true bread-pudding aficionado, agrees.

1 tablespoon unsalted butter, for buttering the pan
7 cups French or Italian bread pieces, torn into 1-inch chunks
3 cups milk
4 eggs
½ cup plus 2 tablespoons sugar
4 large red plums, pitted and cut into ⅛-inch slices (about 1½ cups)
⅛ teaspoon ground cinnamon
1 teaspoon fresh lemon juice
Vanilla ice cream or whipped cream for serving (optional)

1. Preheat the oven to 350°F. Butter a 2-quart or 11¾-by-7½-inch glass or ceramic baking dish.

2. Put the bread in a large bowl, pour the milk over it, and let it sit for about 15 minutes so that the bread absorbs the milk.

3. Beat the eggs with the ½ cup sugar until smooth. Pour the egg mixture into the soaked bread and mix gently. Scrape this mixture into the baking dish.

4. Arrange the plum slices in even rows over the top of the pudding. Mix

together the cinnamon and the remaining 2 tablespoons sugar and sprinkle over the plums. Sprinkle the lemon juice over the plums.

5. Bake for 35 to 40 minutes until the pudding is just lightly browned. Let cool slightly before serving with ice cream or whipped cream, if desired.

Chocolate Madness Cake

Serves 8 to 10

Deliciously sinful, this rich, fudgy cake is for chocolate lovers only. I like to serve it with sliced berries or dollops of unsweetened whipped cream to cut the chocolate intensity. Without question, no frosting is required!

¾ cup unbleached all-purpose flour
1 teaspoon baking powder
6 ounces semisweet chocolate, coarsely chopped
4 ounces unsweetened chocolate, coarsely chopped
¼ cup brewed strong coffee
10 tablespoons (1 stick plus 2 tablespoons) unsalted butter at
room temperature
2 cups granulated sugar
5 eggs, separated, at room temperature
Confectioners' sugar for dusting

1. Preheat the oven to 325°F. Butter and flour a deep 9-inch round cake pan. Line the bottom of the pan with waxed or parchment paper and butter and flour the paper.

2. Whisk together the flour and baking powder.

3. Melt both chocolates with the coffee in a double boiler over hot (not simmering) water, stirring until smooth. Or, put the chocolate and coffee in a microwave-safe container, cover loosely with waxed paper, and microwave on medium (50 percent) power for 2 to 3 minutes until the chocolate is shiny. Remove the container from the microwave and stir the chocolate until smooth and melted. Set the chocolate aside to cool slightly.

4. In a large bowl, using an electric mixer set at medium-high speed, cream the butter and sugar for about 3 minutes until light and fluffy. Beat in the egg yolks, one at a time. Add the flour mixture and beat until combined. The batter will be very thick.

5. In a large, dry, grease-free bowl, using an electric mixer set on medium-high, beat the egg whites until frothy. Increase the speed to high and beat until the whites form stiff, shiny peaks.

6. Fold about a quarter of the chocolate mixture into the whites. When incorporated, fold in the remaining chocolate. Gently fold in the butter-sugar mixture. Do not overmix; fold just until no white streaks are visible.

7. Scrape the batter into the prepared pan and bake about 1 hour and 15 minutes until the top is set and a toothpick inserted in the center comes out with a few moist crumbs. Turn off the oven, open the oven door a few inches, and leave the cake in the oven for 30 minutes.

8. Let it cool on a wire rack, and when still only slightly warm, using a kitchen knife, loosen the cake from the sides of the pan and invert it onto a serving plate. Peel off the waxed paper. Dust the top of the cake with confectioners' sugar and cut into wedges to serve.

Poached Pears in Beaujolais

Serves 6

*Pears are so elegant they are always appropriate for dessert, and this is
a simple way to prepare them. It's especially nice to poach them in the
Beaujolais Nouveau that arrives in the stores in the fall. The young, light,
pleasantly astringent, wine matches well with pears. Depending
on the mood of the party, serve these in a straight-sided glass trifle bowl
or an old-fashioned ceramic pie plate. These are excellent served with
biscotti or almond cookies.*

6 Bosc pears, peeled with stems intact
½ cup sugar
4 cups fruity red wine, such as Beaujolais
⅓ cup crème de cassis
2 tablespoons fresh lemon juice
1 vanilla bean, split lengthwise
6 whole cloves
Fresh mint sprigs for garnish

1. Trim the bottom of the pears so that they can sit upright. Put them in
a large nonaluminum saucepan.

2. Mix the sugar, wine, crème de cassis, and lemon juice together and
pour over the pears. Add the vanilla bean and the cloves.

3. Cover the pan and bring the liquid to a simmer over medium heat.
Simmer, partially covered, for about 30 minutes, turning the pears occasionally until they are cooked through and nicely and evenly colored.

4. Remove the pan from the heat and let the pears cool in the liquid. Transfer both the pears and the liquid to a glass or ceramic bowl. Cover and refrigerate for 24 hours before serving. Garnish with mint sprigs.

winter

mornings

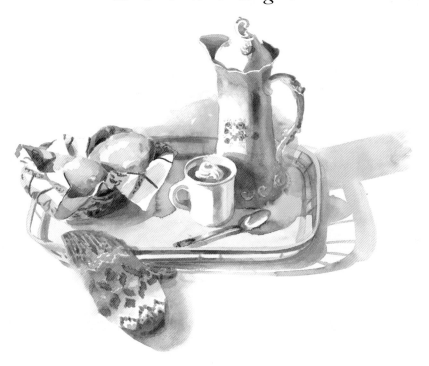

Pancakes with Warm Apple and Pear Topping

Serves 6, makes eighteen to twenty 4-inch pancakes

These are great pancakes for the weekend breakfast cook. They can be whipped up while the apples and pears for the topping slowly cook.

Fruit Topping:
1 tablespoon unsalted butter
3 medium tart apples, peeled, cored, and cut into ½-inch chunks
2 medium pears, peeled, cored, and cut into ½-inch chunks
2 tablespoons sugar

Pancakes:
1¾ cups unbleached all-purpose flour
2 teaspoons sugar
1 teaspoon salt
1½ teaspoons baking powder
1 teaspoon baking soda
2 large eggs
2 cups milk
2 tablespoons unsalted butter, melted

1. To make the fruit topping, melt the butter in a medium skillet. Add the apples and pears and sauté low heat for about 5 minutes. Stir in the sugar, cover the pan, and cook for about 10 minutes longer, occasionally shaking the pan, until the apples and pears are soft. Cover to keep warm.

2. Meanwhile, to make the pancakes, whisk together the flour, sugar, salt, baking powder, and baking soda in a large bowl.

3. In another bowl, beat the eggs lightly and then stir in the milk. Pour into the bowl with the dry ingredients and combine with a few quick strokes using a wooden spoon or rubber spatula. Stir in the melted butter only until mixed. The batter will be slightly lumpy.

4. Heat a large skillet or griddle over high heat. Spray with vegetable oil spray or brush with oil. Spoon about 2 tablespoons of batter onto the skillet for each pancake and cook the pancakes for about 2 to 3 minutes, turning once when the pancakes are golden brown on the bottom, until golden brown on both sides. Stack the cooked pancakes on a heatproof platter and keep warm in a warm (200°F) oven. Continue making pancakes until all the batter is used.

5. Serve the pancakes warm with a spoonful of topping over each one.

French Toast with Citrus Compote

Serves 6

One of the many good things about French toast is that it's best when made with stale bread. This means that one-day-old bread is good, and two-day-old bread is better! I buy good bakery bread for this recipe, and ask the baker for yesterday's loaf. If I can't get it, I simply let the bread sit at room temperature for a day or two. Choose French or Italian bread, sourdough, semolina bread, brioche, or challah. All are terrific. If you use a baguette of French bread, you will probably want three slices per person; if you use a larger loaf, two slices per serving will do. The bread is cooked in an orange and egg batter and served topped with a fresh citrus compote.

French Toast:
6 large eggs
⅓ cup Grand Marnier or other orange-flavored liqueur
2 tablespoons sugar
¼ teaspoon salt
½ cup milk
½ teaspoon vanilla extract
Juice of 2 oranges
12 to 18 slices stale bread (depending on the type used),
cut into ¾-inch-thick slices

Citrus Compote:
4 medium oranges, peeled
2 medium pink grapefruits, peeled
2 tablespoons orange juice
1 tablespoon Grand Marnier or other orange-flavored liqueur
1 tablespoon sugar

3 tablespoons unsalted butter, for cooking

1. To prepare the French toast, in a large mixing bowl, whisk together the eggs, Grand Marnier or other liqueur, sugar, salt, milk, vanilla, and orange juice.

2. Lay the bread slices in a large shallow dish. Pour the egg mixture over the slices and turn them a few times so that they absorb the liquid. Cover with plastic wrap and refrigerate overnight.

3. To make the compote, holding the oranges and then the grapefruit over a large glass or ceramic bowl to catch their juices, divide them into segments. Trim any excess white pith from the segments. Cut the orange and grapefruit segments into 1-inch pieces.

4. Mix together the orange juice, Grand Marnier, and sugar. Pour over the fruit and juices then toss. Set aside while cooking the French toast.

5. Melt about a tablespoon of butter in a large skillet over medium-low heat. Cook the soaked bread slices in batches for 4 to 5 minutes on each side until golden brown, adding more butter as necessary. As several slices are cooked, set them on a heatproof platter in a warm (200°F) oven to keep warm while cooking the rest.

6. Place 2 slices of French toast on each of 6 warm plates and spoon citrus compote over the top of each slice.

Potato Gratin with Scrambled Eggs and Sausage

Serves 6

Potatoes and scrambled eggs are a perfect match, particularly on a chilly winter morning. These are easy to assemble, and while they bake, you can scramble the eggs and broil the sausages so that everything is piping hot at the same time. If the broiler and oven share the same space, cook the sausages in a skillet on top of the stove, following package directions.

6 to 8 baking potatoes (about 3 pounds), peeled and cut crosswise
into ¼-inch-thick slices
Salt and freshly ground black pepper to taste
2 teaspoons crumbled dried sage
1 cup (about 4 ounces) freshly grated Gruyère cheese
½ cup (about 2 ounces) freshly grated Parmesan cheese
1 cup dry white wine
1 cup half-and-half
12 breakfast sausage links or patties
2 tablespoons unsalted butter
10 large eggs, lightly beaten

1. Preheat the oven to 400°F. Butter a 14-by-9-inch gratin or baking dish.

2. Arrange a third of the potato slices in an overlapping pattern in the dish. Season with salt and pepper and sprinkle with one third of the sage. Sprinkle with one third of the cheeses. Repeat twice more to make 3 layers each of potatoes, seasonings, and cheese, ending with cheese.

3. In a small bowl, whisk the wine into the half-and-half. Pour over the potatoes, tilting the dish slightly to distribute the liquid evenly without disturbing the potatoes. Bake for 45 to 50 minutes until the potatoes are tender when pierced with a fork and are golden brown.

4. Preheat the broiler (if it is separate from the oven).

5. About 10 minutes before the potato gratin is done, lay the sausages in a foil-lined broiling pan and broil for 2 to 3 minutes per side until cooked through. Drain on paper towels.

6. Meanwhile, melt the butter in a large skillet over medium heat. Season the eggs with salt and pepper to taste and pour into the hot skillet. Cook, stirring the eggs constantly, until desired doneness.

7. To serve, spoon the scrambled eggs onto a warm platter and arrange the sausages next to them. Serve at once with the potato gratin.

Smoked Salmon Tart

Serves 6

This is one of my all-time favorite tarts. It can easily be made with the ends and trimmings from smoked salmon, which are not as expensive as center slices. Serve it with a green salad, croissants, and Champagne for a special brunch or breakfast.

Buttery Pastry Dough, following
1 large egg white, lightly beaten
4 ounces smoked salmon, sliced
1 cup (4 ounces) grated Swiss cheese
4 large eggs
¾ cup whole milk
½ cup heavy cream
1 tablespoon finely chopped fresh dill
Freshly ground black pepper to taste

1. Roll the pastry dough into a 12-inch circle about ½ inch thick on a sheet of waxed paper or a countertop lightly dusted with flour. Carefully lift the dough and press it into a 10-inch tart pan or 9-inch pie plate. Trim the edges of the dough and crimp them with a fork or your fingertips. Cover the pastry shell with plastic wrap and freeze for 30 minutes.

2. Preheat the oven to 425°F.

3. Take the pastry shell from the freezer and brush it with the egg white. Bake for 5 minutes. Set it aside to cool slightly. Meanwhile, increase the oven temperature to 450°F.

4. Lay the salmon slices over the bottom of the pastry shell and sprinkle with cheese.

5. Beat the eggs, milk, cream, and dill with a fork and season with pepper. Gently pour this mixture over the salmon and cheese. Bake for 15 minutes.

6. Reduce the oven temperature to 350°F and continue baking for 20 to 30 minutes until the top is golden and the custard is set. A 10-inch tart will bake a little faster than a 9-inch pie. Cool slightly before serving.

Buttery Pastry Dough

Makes one 9-inch pie shell or 10-inch tart shell

This pastry is easy to make in the food processor (the method I prefer because it is so quick and fail-safe), but I have given the "old-fashioned" hand method as an alternative.

1 cup unbleached all-purpose flour
½ teaspoon salt
5 tablespoons unsalted butter, chilled and cut into pieces
1½ teaspoons vegetable shortening, chilled
3 to 4 tablespoons ice water, or as needed

1. Put the flour, salt, butter, and shortening in the bowl of a food processor fitted with the metal blade.

2. Pulse the food processor 4 to 5 times to break up the fat. With the food processor running, add 3 tablespoons ice water. Turn the food processor off, and then pulse it 5 or 6 times. The dough should begin to mass on the blade. If not, add 1 tablespoon water, or more as needed. When the dough holds together in a cohesive mass, it is done; do not overmix.

3. Turn the dough out onto the countertop. Flatten it with the palm of your hand, dust it lightly with flour, and wrap the dough in plastic wrap or waxed paper. Chill for 1 to 2 hours before rolling out according to directions in the tart recipe.

Old-Fashioned Method:

1. In a large bowl, whisk together the flour and salt. Using a knife, a pastry blender, or your fingertips, blend the chilled butter and shortening into the dry ingredients until the mixture resembles coarse crumbs.

2. Sprinkle 1 tablespoon of the ice water over the flour and toss to distribute evenly. Add more water, 1 tablespoon at a time, tossing until the dough holds together when pressed between your·fingertips. Gather it into a cohesive mass.

3. Turn the dough out onto the countertop. Flatten it with the palm of your hand into a disk shape, dust it lightly with flour, and wrap the dough in plastic wrap or waxed paper. Chill for 1 to 2 hours before rolling out according to directions in the tart recipe.

Swiss Chard Frittata

Serves 6

Swiss chard is a versatile green with a delicious, earthy flavor and, like most greens, is easy to find during the colder months. I cook chard several ways: I sauté it in olive oil, add it to light, creamy casseroles, toss it with pasta, or stir it into soup. But I especially like to pair it with eggs in a simple frittata. It's just the thing on a cold winter morning served with bacon and hot coffee—and is great for a breakfast or brunch party, as it is easy to assemble and bakes in less than 30 minutes. And because frittata can be served at room temperature, it can wait until your guests are at the table.

1 large bunch (about 1½ pounds) green Swiss chard, stemmed
1 tablespoon unsalted butter
1 tablespoon extra-virgin olive oil
1 tablespoon minced shallot
2 tablespoons minced onion
5 large eggs
¼ cup half-and-half
¼ teaspoon ground nutmeg
Salt and freshly ground black pepper to taste
2½ ounces Gruyère cheese, cut into ½-inch cubes (about ½ cup)
3 tablespoons freshly grated Parmesan cheese

1. Preheat the oven to 350°F.

2. Put the chard in a vegetable steamer over boiling water, cover, and cook over medium heat for 8 to 10 minutes until tender. Drain well, chop coarsely, and set aside.

3. Heat the butter and oil in a large skillet over medium-high heat until foaming. When the foam begins to subside, add the shallot and onion and cook for 2 to 3 minutes just until translucent. Stir in the chopped chard, mix well, and remove from the heat.

4. Butter a 10-inch round glass or ceramic baking dish or an 11¾-by-7½-inch rectangular glass baking dish. Spread the Swiss chard mixture evenly in the dish.

5. In a bowl, combine the eggs, half-and-half, and nutmeg and season with salt and pepper. Beat thoroughly and pour over the chard. Dot with the cubed cheese, pressing the pieces into the egg mixture slightly, and sprinkle with Parmesan. Bake for 25 to 30 minutes, until the top is lightly browned.

6. Let cool slightly and serve warm, or serve at room temperature.

Smoked Chicken and Apple Hash

Serves 6

This is a sensational hash to serve with poached or scrambled eggs. I find I have to cook it in two skillets, but if you have an extra-large skillet, you may not have to use two. Specialty shops and some butchers carry smoked chicken breasts, but if they're unavailable, use poached skinned chicken breasts or substitute smoked turkey meat for the chicken. Remember that the pinkness near the bone of smoked poultry is natural and does not indicate that it is undercooked. As you cook the hash, the pinkness will disappear.

4 medium unpeeled red new potatoes, cut into ½-inch dice
(about 4 cups)
1 tablespoon unsalted butter
1 tablespoon extra-virgin olive oil
2 cloves garlic, thinly sliced
1 cup finely chopped onion
1 fennel bulb, cut into ½-inch dice
1 rib celery, cut into ½-inch dice (about ½ cup)
2 unpeeled Granny Smith apples, cored, and cut into 1-inch chunks
6 ounces fresh mushrooms, stemmed and thinly sliced (about 2 cups)
2 smoked whole chicken breasts (about 2 pounds), boned and cut into
1-inch chunks (about 3½ cups)
Salt and freshly ground black pepper to taste
½ cup chopped fresh parsley

1. Bring a large pot of lightly salted water to a boil. Boil the potatoes for 10 to 15 minutes just until tender. Drain and set aside.

2. Divide the butter and oil between 2 large nonstick skillets and heat over medium-high heat. Add the garlic, onion, fennel, and celery and cook for about 5 minutes, stirring occasionally. Add the apples and mushrooms and cook an additional 5 minutes.

3. Add the chicken pieces and cooked potatoes. Season with salt and pepper. Cook over medium heat for 20 to 25 minutes, turning occasionally with a spatula, until the hash is cooked through and slightly crusted. Stir in the fresh parsley and adjust the seasoning. Serve immediately.

Winter Fruits Salad
with Endive and Walnuts

Serves 6

*I consider this a Waldorf salad, because it contains apples and walnuts. But
I have to admit the similarities stop there. This contemporary salad boasts
some of the best wintertime fruits and is a fine first course or side dish at
brunch—plus it is equally at home later in the day accompanying roast
chicken or grilled steak.*

⅓ cup apple cider
2 tablespoons dried cranberries
2 heads endive (about 2½ cups leaves)
2 bunches watercress, stemmed (about 4 loosely packed cups)
1 medium unpeeled red apple, cored and cut into 1-inch pieces
1 unpeeled Bosc pear, cored and cut into 1-inch pieces
2 tablespoons Dijon mustard
1 tablespoon white wine vinegar
1 teaspoon fresh lemon juice
½ cup extra-virgin olive oil
1 large unpeeled red apple
½ cup walnut halves, lightly toasted (see Note, page 61)
2 ounces fresh goat cheese, crumbled

1. In a small saucepan, warm the cider over medium-high heat until hot
but not boiling. Remove from the heat and add the cranberries. Let the
cranberries macerate in the cider for 20 to 30 minutes.

2. Tear the endive leaves in half and place in a large bowl. Add the
watercress, chopped apple, and chopped pear and toss to combine.

3. In a small bowl, whisk the mustard, vinegar, and lemon juice together. Slowly add the olive oil, whisking constantly, until the vinaigrette thickens.

4. Cut the apple into thin wedges.

5. Toss about ⅓ cup of the vinaigrette with the salad and heap the salad into a large shallow bowl or platter. Sprinkle the walnut halves and crumbled cheese over the top. Drain the cranberries and sprinkle them over the top. Garnish with the apple wedges and drizzle with the remaining vinaigrette, if desired. Serve immediately.

Apricot and Pecan Scones

Makes 8 to 10 scones

*Rich and delicious, these scones can be assembled and baked in no time.
I assure you that the aroma of the baking scones will roust anyone from
under a comforter on a chilly morning.*

2 cups unbleached all-purpose flour
¼ cup packed light brown sugar
1 tablespoon baking powder
¼ teaspoon salt
½ cup (about 2½ ounces) dried apricots, finely chopped
¼ cup finely chopped pecans
1 cup heavy cream
¼ cup milk
1 large egg white, lightly beaten
1 to 2 teaspoons granulated sugar

1. Preheat the oven to 425°F. Spray a baking sheet with vegetable oil
spray or line it with parchment paper.

2. In a large bowl, whisk together the flour, brown sugar, baking powder,
and salt. Add the apricots and pecans. Slowly stir in the cream and milk to
form a sticky dough.

3. Turn the dough out onto a well-floured surface and, using a lightly
floured rolling pin, roll it into a 9-inch circle about ¾ inch thick.

4. Stamp out scones using a 2- or 2½-inch biscuit cutter or an overturned glass. Place the scones about 1 inch apart on the prepared baking sheet. Gather the scraps, re-roll, and make more scones.

5. Brush the tops of the scones with egg white and sprinkle them with sugar. Bake for 15 to 20 minutes until golden brown. Serve warm or at room temperature.

Cranberry-Walnut Muffins

Makes 12

Bursting with the flavors of tart cranberries and sweet walnuts, these muffins are delicious for breakfast or later in the day. The cranberries make them especially nice for the holidays; their overall warm sweetness makes them perfect any time of year. I like to serve these piled in a basket lined with a cheerful red-checked napkin.

2 cups unbleached all-purpose flour
2 teaspoons baking powder
½ teaspoon baking soda
½ teaspoon salt
1 cup fresh or frozen cranberries
½ cup walnut halves, toasted (see Note)
½ cup granulated sugar
½ cup packed light brown sugar
½ cup (1 stick) unsalted butter, melted
½ cup milk
1 large egg, lightly beaten
1 teaspoon vanilla extract

1. Preheat the oven to 400°F. Lightly butter 12 standard-sized muffin cups (each cup about 3 inches in diameter across the top). Or, line the muffin cups with paper liners.

2. In a large bowl, whisk together the flour, baking powder, baking soda, and salt.

3. Put the cranberries, walnuts, and sugars in a food processor fitted with a metal blade. Pulse 8 to 10 times until coarsely ground. Alternatively, finely chop the cranberries and walnuts and toss them with the sugars.

4. Combine the butter, milk, egg, and vanilla. Pour into the flour mixture and stir until just combined. Scrape the cranberry-walnut mixture into the batter and mix until just combined. Do not overmix.

5. Spoon the batter into the muffin cups, filling each one about two-thirds full. Bake for 15 to 20 minutes until the muffins are risen, browned, and a toothpick inserted in the center of one comes out clean.

6. Set the muffin tins on wire racks and let the muffins cool in the cups for about 5 minutes. Turn the muffins out onto the racks to cool completely.

Note: To toast the walnuts, spread them on a baking sheet and toast them in a preheated 350°F oven or toaster oven for about 5 minutes until golden brown and fragrant. Shake the pan once or twice for even toasting. Slide the nuts off the baking sheet as soon as they reach the desired color to halt the cooking and let them cool.

Old-Fashioned Hot Chocolate

Serves 6

Hot chocolate made by melting solid chocolate is richer and creamier than hot chocolate made from cocoa. I love to make this for my girls after a morning on the sledding hill or at the ice rink. It also is a luscious way to begin the day.

6 cups whole or low-fat milk
9 tablespoons sugar
3 ounces unsweetened chocolate, finely chopped
1½ teaspoons pure vanilla extract
Whipped cream for garnish (optional)

In a medium saucepan, heat the milk, sugar, and chocolate over medium heat, stirring constantly. When the chocolate is melted and the mixture is nearly boiling, remove from the heat. Stir in the vanilla. Pour the hot chocolate into mugs. Top with whipped cream, if desired.

Winter White Hot Chocolate

Serves 6

Sweet, rich, and seductive, hot chocolate made with creamy white chocolate is an elegant drink to sip on frosty mornings. This recipe makes six steaming cups; you can reduce the amounts for fewer servings. White chocolate is more heat sensitive than dark chocolate and must be cooked very gently.

6 cups whole milk
9 ounces white chocolate, finely chopped
2 tablespoons pure vanilla extract
Whipped cream for garnish (optional)

In a medium saucepan, heat the milk to simmering over medium heat. Lower the heat to medium-low and stir in the chocolate and vanilla. Cook until hot but not boiling, stirring frequently. Remove the pan from the heat and pour into mugs. Top with whipped cream, if desired.

Winter Spice Tea

Serves 6

Hot spiced tea is a bracing drink, particularly on chilly mornings. When spiked with rum, it is transformed into a delightful brunch drink.

4 cups freshly brewed English or Irish Breakfast tea,
or any orange pekoe tea
¼ cup sugar
2 cinnamon sticks
10 whole cloves
½ lemon, sliced into rounds
½ orange, sliced into rounds
⅓ cup dark rum (optional)

1. Strain the tea into a large saucepan. Bring to a gentle simmer over medium-high heat.

2. Add the sugar, cinnamon sticks, cloves, and all but 6 of the lemon and orange slices. Simmer for 5 minutes. Remove the pan from the heat, cover, and let stand for 10 minutes to give the flavors time to meld. Stir in the rum, if desired.

3. Strain the tea into large teacups and float the reserved lemon and orange slices on top. Serve at once.

Mocha Coffee

Serves 6

Chocolate-flavored coffee hits the spot on cold mornings, particularly when laced with brandy. With or without the spirits, this is a soothing and warming drink.

1½ cups whole milk
1½ teaspoons unsweetened cocoa powder
1 tablespoon sugar
¼ cup brandy (optional)
3 cups hot freshly brewed coffee
Whipped cream for garnish (optional)

In a medium saucepan, heat the milk over medium heat. Stir in the cocoa and sugar until they are dissolved and the mixture is steaming but not boiling. Add the brandy, if desired. Slowly pour the hot coffee into the milk mixture, stirring constantly. Ladle the coffee into warm coffee cups and top with whipped cream, if desired.

Bloody Marys
with Fresh Horseradish and Lemon

Serves 6

What is brunch without Bloody Marys? This recipe comes from the bar at Nick and Eddie, a wonderful New York neighborhood restaurant. It makes the best Bloody Mary I have ever tasted.

1 cup canned tomatoes with juice
3 tablespoons thinly sliced red onion
1 tablespoon thinly sliced pimiento (canned roasted red peppers)
2 cloves garlic, sliced
2 tablespoons white vinegar
3 tablespoons Worcestershire sauce
2 tablespoons Tabasco sauce
1 tablespoon prepared horseradish
Pinch red pepper flakes
1 teaspoon sugar
Salt and freshly ground black pepper to taste
3 cups tomato juice
6 ounces (¾ cup) vodka
Juice of ½ lemon
Freshly grated horseradish for garnish
6 lemon slices for garnish

1. Put the canned tomatoes and their juice, onions, pimiento, garlic, vinegar, Worcestershire sauce, Tabasco, prepared horseradish, red pepper flakes, and sugar in a blender or a food processor fitted with the metal blade. Season with salt and pepper. Blend or process until smooth. Pour into a large pitcher.

2. Add the tomato juice, vodka, and lemon juice and stir well. Pour over ice cubes in large glasses and garnish with fresh horseradish and lemon slices.

Pineapple Royal Fizzes

Serves 6

When I'm Caribbean dreamin', I like to whip up a batch of these frothy drinks. Regardless of the wintry weather, everyone's mood gets sunnier.

2 cups pineapple juice
1 cup orange juice
¾ cup white rum
¼ cup plus 2 tablespoons Triple Sec or Cointreau
½ cup seltzer or club soda
8 ice cubes
6 fresh round pineapple slices for garnish

1. Combine the pineapple juice, orange juice, rum, Triple Sec or Cointreau, seltzer or soda, and ice cubes in a blender. Blend at high speed until smooth and frothy.

2. Pour into tall chilled glasses and garnish with pineapple slices. Serve at once.

Fresh Citrus Mimosas

Serves 6; makes 12 mimosas

I welcome weekend brunch guests with this festive version of the traditional mimosa. First, I put the Champagne on to chill and then I squeeze the fresh oranges and grapefruits so that the drinks are ready to assemble as soon as the party begins.

12 oranges
3 pink or ruby red grapefruits
Two 750-ml bottles Champagne, chilled

1. Squeeze the oranges and grapefruits. Combine the juices in a large pitcher and chill. You will have about 6 cups of juice.

2. Pour half of the juice into Champagne flutes and add an equal amount of Champagne. Serve at once.

RECIPE INDEX

TABLE OF EQUIVALENTS

The exact equivalents in the following tables have been rounded for convenience.

OVEN TEMPERATURES

Fahrenheit	Celsius	Gas
250	120	½
275	140	1
300	150	2
325	160	3
350	180	4
375	190	5
400	200	6
425	220	7
450	230	8
475	240	9
500	260	10

WEIGHTS

US/UK	Metric
1 oz	30 g
2 oz	60 g
3 oz	90 g
4 oz (¼ lb)	125 g
5 oz (⅓ lb)	155 g
6 oz	185 g
7 oz	220 g
8 oz (½ lb)	250 g
10 oz	315 g
12 oz (¾ lb)	375 g
14 oz	440 g
16 oz (1 lb)	500 g
1½ lb	750 g
2 lb	1 kg
3 lb	1.5 kg

LENGTH MEASURES

⅛ in	3 mm
¼ in	6 mm
½ in	12 mm
1 in	2.5 cm
2 in	5 cm
3 in	7.5 cm
4 in	10 cm
5 in	13 cm
6 in	15 cm
7 in	18 cm
8 in	20 cm
9 in	23 cm
10 in	25 cm
11 in	28 cm
12 in	30 cm

LIQUIDS

US	Metric	UK
2 tbl	30 ml	1 fl oz
¼ cup	60 ml	2 fl oz
⅓ cup	80 ml	3 fl oz
½ cup	125 ml	4 fl oz
⅔ cup	160 ml	5 fl oz
¾ cup	180 ml	6 fl oz
1 cup	250 ml	8 fl oz
1½ cup	375 ml	12 fl oz
2 cups	500 ml	16 fl oz
4 cups/1qt	1 liter	32 fl oz